AF584314

P. Crumble and Jonathan Bentley

We Are All Strong

An Omnibus Book from Scholastic Australia

We are all **STRONG**

Our world changes fast.

Look to the future,

let go of the past.

We are all **STRONG**

You can't always win.

Be proud of yourself,

draw strength from within.

We are all **STRONG**

We all make mistakes.

Be ready to learn,

your spirit won't break.

We are all **STRONG**

Let go of your fears.

The road to success

is often not clear.

We are all **STRONG**

You're caring and brave.

Others take your lead

in how to behave.

We are all **STRONG**

But as hard as we try

sometimes we stumble,

it's okay to cry.

We are all **STRONG**

Your strength is a gift.

Look out for someone

who might need a lift.

We are all **STRONG**

Friends come and go.

You never know when

a friendship will grow.

We are all **STRONG**

There's good and bad days.

We will accept when

we don't get our way.

We are all **STRONG**

Life's twists can be great.

Good things can take time.

Sometimes we must wait.

We are all **STRONG**

We live our life true.

Believe in yourself.

Let your light shine through!

To AR and Alex who are my strength—PC

For M—JB

Omnibus Books
an imprint of Scholastic Australia Pty Ltd (ABN 11 000 614 577)
PO Box 579, Gosford NSW 2250.
www.scholastic.com.au

Part of the Scholastic Group
Sydney · Auckland · New York · Toronto · London · Mexico City ·
New Delhi · Hong Kong · Buenos Aires · Puerto Rico

Published by Scholastic Australia in 2022.

ISBN 978-1-76112-783-0

A catalogue record for this book is available from the National Library of Australia

Typeset in Austral Slab.

Illustrations created using pencil and watercolours.

Printed in China by RR Donnelley.

Scholastic Australia's policy, in association with RR Donnelley, is to use papers that are renewable and made efficiently from wood grown in responsibly managed forests, so as to minimise its environmental footprint.

10 9 8 7 6 5 24 25 26 27 28 / 2